# How to Choose "Just Right" Books:

# Helping Kids Grow as Readers

## Becky Spence

ThisReadingMama.com

How to Choose "Just Right" Books: Helping Kids Grow as Readers

## This book is dedicated to:

First and foremost, my Heavenly Father above. Without Him, I would be nothing. He has opened amazing doors along this journey and given me encouragement, creativity, and passion. Thank You!

My husband, who is my biggest supporter. Thank you for loving on our children while I worked a few hours here and there to finish this project. I love you!

My four little blessings. You are a huge part of my inspiration. I love being your mommy and your teacher, through the ups and downs.

Dr. Francine Johnston. Thank you for using your passion of teaching to inspire me to do great things.

# TABLE OF CONTENTS

# TABLE OF CONTENTS (Continued)

## INTRODUCTION

We all want our kids to grow as readers, becoming confident and independent. Giving kids a balanced diet of reading, writing, and spelling will do just this. But the activities and reading we ask them to do must be on a level that is challenging enough to foster growth without frustrating or boring them. This is true of any literacy activity, especially reading. Many call it the "just right" reading level. But what constitutes a "just right" book? What factors go into figuring out a "just right" book anyway? That's exactly what this book is designed to help you do.

The goal of this book is to equip parents, teachers, or tutors in finding "just right" books for young readers. One commonly used strategy used for finding a child's reading level is by having a child read through a list of words out of context. Although doing this may help you find the child's starting point, I believe the only true way to find that "just right" level is to listen to the child read. Another popular method is the five-finger rule. It goes a little something like this: Ask your child to read one page of text. If he misses 0-1 words, the book is too easy. If he misses 2-

3 words, the book is "just right". If he misses 4-5 words, the book is too hard. In my opinion, the five-finger rule also falls short in helping both teachers and parents pinpoint a child's reading level with accuracy. For example, the five-finger rule does not take into account how many words are on the page, how quickly the child is reading those words, or if the child can even remember what he has just read. All of these are important factors in picking "just right" books.

Before we jump in too deep, I want to make this point clear: "Just right" books are books that readers can both read AND comprehend. Naturally, we know that if a young reader cannot read the words, a book may be too hard. However, I often hear parents say their child can read on a fourth grade level, as the child may be able to say the words on a fourth grade level, but in actuality, the child cannot understand what she is reading. If the child cannot both read AND comprehend the text on a fourth grade level, the child is not reading on that grade level.

While some of the strategies I introduce in this book might be on the technical side, I will strive to show how finding "just right" books for readers is both practical and helpful. Despite some of the math required in calculating percentages, finding the right books for your child is not a formula. There are many other factors included, which we will touch on as well.

I am excited to begin this journey with you and pray that the ideas and teachings in this book will help you be successful in finding "just right" books so that your young reader can be successful in growing as a confident and independent reader.

## Chapter 1: THE IMPORTANCE OF
## "JUST RIGHT" TEXTS

Does a mother expect her one-month old to learn to walk? Do we hand our five-year old the key to the car and ask him to drive to the store? Would a swim instructor teach a beginning swimmer by launching him into the deep end? Of course, the answer to these questions is a resounding, "Absolutely not!" We all know that one-month olds are *not ready* to walk, five-year olds are *not ready* to drive, and a beginning swimmer is *not ready* to conquer the deep end. Not ready. When a child is not ready, learning is at its lowest. On the flip side, learning happens most effectively when a child *is ready* for a specific strategy or skill. This applies to reading as well.

When we consistently place readers in texts that are too hard (or even too easy) for them, we have a problem. New learning does not thrive in these zones. Rather, learning happens in the *Zone of Proximal Development*, or the child's "just right" level, as first introduced by Vygotsky. "When students are instructed within their own zone of proximal development—at their own level— they are able to build on what they already know, to learn what they need to know next, to move forward" (Bear, et al. 2004). "Just right" texts are just enough out of reach for the young reader so that adult support is needed. Once the support is given, the child is able to read and comprehend the text by himself. This level is where new learning takes place and boredom or frustration is at its lowest.

Not only do readers need to have a steady diet of reading on their "just right" level because it fosters new learning, but there is also another very important factor involved here: motivation. Many of the struggling readers I have taught over the years have said, "I can't read" before the book was ever opened. Many, because they had spent so much time frustrated in books that were too hard for them, began to believe they could not read anymore. **Motivation is so vital to the learner that I would be tempted to rate it as the most important factor in learning to read.** It is like the battery that gives energy to the attitude. Lack of motivation encourages kids to shut down and avoid reading altogether. I do not blame them. Why would any sane person purposely expose himself to working at his frustration level day

after day after day? Giving readers books on their "just right"
level begins to build confidence and motivation. That "I can do
it!" attitude can return. I have seen it happen first-hand.

## Chapter 2: THE THREE READING LEVELS

We all know the story of *Goldilocks and the Three Bears*. Goldilocks barges into the three bears' home unannounced. She samples their porridge, sits in their chairs, and tries out their beds. The three familiar phrases that are repeated in the story are *too hard*, *too soft*, and *just right*. These phrases are fitting when it comes to reading as well. When a child picks up a book, it is either *too hard*, *too soft* (easy), or *just right*. While we want to spend most of our instructional time teaching with "just right" books, each kind of book does serve a purpose. In this chapter, we will explore the Easy (Independent) Level, Too Hard (Frustration) Level, and the "Just Right" (Instructional) Level. Chapter 8 will focus in on how to calculate these levels using some simple math combined with reading observations and behaviors.

### Easy (Independent Level)

An easy book for a child is one in which he can a) read the words **and** b) understand *without* help. Easy books may be books you have already read and discussed with a child, but now he can read and comprehend them without your support.

**Easy books should be used for**

- independent work,

- homework,

- silent reading time (I call it "independent reading time"),

- building fluency, and

- building confidence.

**Just Right (Instructional Level)**

A "just right" book is one that a child can a) read and b) understand *with* minimal support from an adult. "Just right" books help the reader grow in his reading and comprehension by introducing new words and new strategies in a challenging, yet appropriate way.

**"Just right" books should be used for**

- instructional work (with an adult there to provide support),

- learning a new comprehension strategy, and

- learning a new decoding or word strategy for figuring out unknown words.

## Too Hard (Frustration Level)

A book is too hard for a reader when he struggles greatly to a) read and/or b) comprehend, even when provided with support from an adult. Although the book is too hard for the child, there are actually strategic uses for these kinds of books.

### Too hard books should be used for

- Read aloud time. When a child is just learning to read, the too easy and "just right" books for them are mainly simple readers, because they have very few words on each page. If these are the only texts young readers are being exposed to, reading can become boring and uninteresting. Most parents naturally read books aloud that are too hard for their children. Parents can and should read good literature aloud for enjoyment (fiction, non-fiction, poetry, Dr. Seuss, etc.) that the child cannot read and/or comprehend on his own.

- Enjoyment. Most children go through phases during which they hone in on a particular passion for something. When my son wants to pick out a book about trains at the library, I'm not going to respond with, "Oh, you can't pick that book, honey. It's not on your 'just right' level." No way! If all he does is look at the pictures for enjoyment, so be it. By allowing him to explore a book that's of high interest to him, (but just happens to be too hard for him to read on his own), I am instilling in him that reading is *not* just about saying the words correctly and answering difficult questions. It is also about enjoyment.

## Chapter 3: THREE FACTORS THAT DETERMINE "JUST RIGHT" TEXTS

There are two main areas most reading researchers and specialists agree on that can help you determine a reader's "just right" level: 1) word recognition and 2) comprehension. Word recognition AND comprehension have to work together to help determine that "just right" level. While we'll talk about these in length, I also want to entertain a third vital factor in determining what "just right" is for a child: the child's interest.

**Word Recognition (Speed and Accuracy)**

**Here are questions you want to consider when evaluating word recognition:**

- How quickly does the child read the words?

- Does the child read the words with accuracy?

- Does the child rely heavily on context to figure out words?

- Does the child use the punctuation marks to help him read with expression and phrasing?

## Comprehension (Understanding)

**Here are questions you want to consider when evaluating comprehension:**

- Can the child answer questions about the text?

- What kinds of questions can the child answer (only literal questions or is she able to read between the lines a bit to infer)?

- Is the child familiar with the structure (or organization) of the text?

- Are there too many words that the child does not understand, even if he can read them correctly?

- Is the child using comprehension strategies before, during, and after reading?

## The Child's Interests

**When children are interested in what they are reading, they are more likely to**

- **Stick with it, even if it is a bit challenging.** "Children as well as adults who are interested in particular activities or topics pay closer attention, persist for longer periods of time, learn more, and enjoy their involvement to a greater degree than individuals without such interest" (Allington, 2004).

- **Have the prior knowledge needed to comprehend the text.** Readers have a very hard time making connections, predicting, making mental images, inferring, etc. when they do not possess the prior knowledge related to the topic or theme. In other words, comprehension strategies that good readers use rely heavily on prior knowledge.

- **Understand the vocabulary included in the text.** Because vocabulary words tend to be specific to a certain topic, children who know and love a particular topic (like sharks) will already know most of the vocabulary words before opening the text.

- **Be motivated to read.** Remember that motivation is half the battle with reading!

### Questions to ask to find a child's interests are

- What subject (or subjects) does the child like best in school?

- What are the child's interests outside of school?

- What kinds of toys does the child like to play with?

- Does the child have a hobby (collecting rocks, riding a bike, etc.)?

- What kind of texts does the child like to listen to when an adult reads out loud?

### What About Struggling or Advanced Readers?

If you are teaching a struggling or advanced reader, picking "just right" books can be particularly tricky. Why? While the words and vocabulary may be appropriate for a struggling fifth grader who is reading on a second grade level, the content and look of that second grade book may be too "baby-ish". On the flip side, a third grader may be able to read and comprehend on an eighth grade level, but do I want that third grader to read the content available in some of those texts?

## Struggling Readers: Motivation and Resources

Finding texts for advanced readers can be a challenge, but those who are teaching struggling readers have multiple obstacles to overcome. To me, the two biggest obstacles are lack of motivation and lack of texts that appeal to the struggling reader. Older students who struggle to read are well aware of their weaknesses. They know where they stand in regards to their classmates, friends, or even siblings. Many disguise it by saying things like, "Reading is dumb." This is only code for "I've given up. Help me."

Struggling readers can also lack motivation for an entirely different reason. This reason is outside of their control. While texts they *can* read are plenty, texts they *want* to read are not. As

I have worked with struggling readers over the years, one thing I have noticed is how difficult it can be to find texts appealing to them that are on their reading level.

**How do you get kids to read texts they can and want to read at the same time? Listed below are a few suggestions.**

- **Re-type the text to make it more appealing.** Sometimes the large size of the text or having too many pictures can turn a child off to it. These features can make a book look "baby-ish". Try re-typing the story, excluding the pictures, and presenting it to the child.

- **Pick realistic fiction.** The fact that unrealistic things happen in the text can make it seem like a "baby book". Kids need texts to which they can relate. One of my absolute favorite realistic fiction book series for struggling readers in the third/fourth grade is Cam Jansen. Why? Because the main character is in the fifth grade, meaning she is the same age or older than the struggling reader, which gives it some credibility.

- **Read poetry.** Poetry is great for many reasons. The reason that probably matters most to struggling readers is that it is shorter in length. Some of my favorite poetry to read with struggling readers is written by Shel Silverstein because he makes reading fun. His pictures aren't too baby-ish. Some are even quite gruesome. I would level most of his poetry on a first/second grade level (based on his three of his poetry books: <u>Where the Sidewalk Ends</u>, <u>Falling Up</u>, & <u>A Light in the Attic</u>).

- **Pair the struggling reader up with a younger child.** If the struggling reader (a third grader) reads aloud to a younger child (a first grader) weekly, the third grader would have an authentic reason to practice reading texts on the first grade level. He would also have an "out" if he needed to tell his friends why he's toting around those <u>Frog and Toad</u> books. By the way, this is an authentic way to get the struggling reader to re-read texts for fluency purposes, too!

- **Pick text topics that are of high interest to the child.** I would not last long in a nuclear physics book, even if it was on my reading level! It is of no interest to me. On the flip side, if a student is highly knowledgeable or interested in a certain topic (let's say dinosaurs), he may be able to read texts on a higher level as he will most likely already know a lot of the language and content, which will make the text easier for him.

- **Offer appropriate text choices.** Appropriate choices are texts that the struggling reader can read and wants to read. It does not do any good to offer choices that are too difficult for the child. "Pigeon holing" the child into reading only one kind of book, like Accelerated Reader books, is also not the best idea for struggling readers. Struggling readers enjoy variety, just like everyone else.

- **Read comic books** like <u>Calvin and Hobbs</u> or <u>Toon Books</u>.

- **Read graphic novels** like <u>Sport's Illustrated Graphic Novels</u> (2nd/3rd grade level).

- **Find high interest/ low vocabulary books (a.k.a. hi-lo books)** like <u>High Noon Books</u>. The I Survived Series (2nd/3rd grade level) is another high interest/low vocabulary book series for struggling readers.

- **Read magazines.** For example, <u>Time for Kids</u> has their magazines leveled by grade. My past experience with <u>Time for Kids</u> has been that they use much of the same content for grades 1-6. The vocabulary is just lower for the younger grades. With <u>Time for Kids</u>, you are still getting great content with the added benefit of vocabulary for the struggling reader. <u>God's World News</u> also separates their subscriptions by grade level. Some other good non-fiction magazines might include <u>National Geographic for Kids</u> or <u>Kids Discover</u>.

- **Use online resources like** <u>Scholastic Book Wizard</u>. Click on "Search by Reading Level". If a child is reading on a first grade level, you can check the range 1.0 to 1.9 under

"Grade Level" (see Chapter 7 for book level information). Once you click "Find", look on the left sidebar under the heading "Browse By". Click on the reader's actual grade level under "Interest Level". For example, if the child is in the fourth grade, click on "Grades 3-5". This will give you a decent selection of books that are on a first grade level but are on the interest level of a third through fifth grader.

- **Check your public library.** Some public libraries may have hi-lo reading lists available.

## Chapter 4: WORD RECOGNITION IN CONTEXT

One of the most accurate ways that we can determine if a text is right for a child is to listen to him read the text out loud. "A careful record of a child's oral reading is the best 'window' we can have into the developing reading process" (Morris, 2005). I will explore what this looks like in Chapter 8, but first I want to delve a little deeper to explain exactly what we're looking for as we listen to the child read. In one word: fluency. Broken down, fluency includes these three things:

- reading speed,

- word accuracy, and

- reading with expression.

**Reading Speed**

Can the child read most words within one second (by sight) or does she have to stop many times and sound out words? This question is important because "if reading is not fluent, then comprehension usually suffers" (McKenna & Stahl, 2003). If a child has to focus so much brain power on figuring out words, the brain has a hard time multi-tasking and also figuring out meaning from the words. On the flip side, reading too fast can be detrimental to comprehension. Sometimes children read too fast to attend to meaning, especially the deeper meanings of text. (Valencia & Buly, 2004)

Remember that reading rate is affected by many factors. The rate of reading depends on the purpose of the reading, the mode of reading (oral versus silent), the age of the reader, reading skill, and processing speeds. (Leslie & Caldwell, 2006)

Here is a suggested *words per minute* range, listed by grade level of the text:

Words Per Minute for Grades Kindergarten through Fifth Grade

| Grade Level of Text | Words Per Minute |
|---------------------|------------------|
| Kindergarten | 30 - 65 words |
| First Grade | 40 - 80 words |
| Second Grade | 45 - 90 words |
| Third Grade | 50 - 100 words |
| Fourth Grade | 60 - 120 words |
| Fifth Grade | 70 - 140 words |

Adapted from Leslie & Caldwell (2006)

In chapter 8, we will explore how to calculate words per minute for your reader using a simple math formula.

**Word Accuracy**

Reading speed does not mean much if the child misreads most of the words in the text. This is where word accuracy comes into play. Not only do we want our readers to read at a good rate, we also want them to be able to read the words *with accuracy*. When listening to them read out loud, there are some common mistakes they will make, as you will see in the following list.

**Some common miscues with oral reading are**

1. leaving out or skipping over a word (omissions),

2. adding extra words (insertions),

3. substituting or replacing a word with a different word (sometimes the substitutions make sense, sometimes they do not),

4. repeating a word or phrase over and over,

5. pausing in between words (hesitation),

6. word is read by the adult because the pause is so long. (My rule of thumb is if the child pauses longer than 3-4 seconds, I supply the word out loud.),

7. reading through punctuation, and

8. self-correcting (going back and rereading text in order to correct the original mistake).

(List adapted from McKenna & Stahl, 2003)

When I count how many miscues a child has made in his oral reading, I only count off for the miscues mentioned in numbers 1, 2, 3, and 6 in the list above. (We'll talk more about miscues in Chapter 7.) If a child self-corrects, meaning he re-reads what he just misread and corrects the mistake upon re-reading, I do not count it against him for word accuracy, although some may disagree on this point. Self-corrections will, however, negatively affect reading speed. I do make a note if the child makes a noticeable number of self-corrections, as this could be an indication that the child is relying too heavily on context to help him figure out words versus knowing them by sight. This could be a red flag that the book is too hard for him at this time.

If a child consistently makes the same mistake reading a word *and it does not change the meaning of the text*, I only count it as one mistake. For example, if the child reads *KITTY* for *kitten* throughout the entire book, I only count that as one mistake against him. If, however, the child says CAT one time and KITTY another time, I would count each as a separate mistake. This is particularly important to note with shorter texts. For example, if the text is only 100 words total and *kitten* appears 10 times in the text, it would not be an accurate gauge of the child's word accuracy if I counted off each time she read *KITTY* instead of *kitten*. Please note that names are sometimes hard for kids to read because names do not always follow the "rules" and generalizations of the English language. If the name of the character is an unusual name to your child, like Juan, it is a good idea to use the name in your introduction to the book. For example, in introducing a book with Juan as the main character, you may choose to say, "Today, you're going to read a book about a boy named Juan."

Chapters 7 and 8 will address how to score and level word accuracy.

**Reading with Expression**

Reading with expression means that the child is "reading the text in such a way that it sounds like the spoken word" (Eckenwiler & Eckenwiler, 2007). This includes chunking words into meaningful phrases, paying attention to punctuation, and reading with certain inflections in the voice. Fluency is a process and develops more fully as readers become familiar with the text. It often does not appear upon the first reading of a text. However, it is still important to make notes as to how the young reader integrates fluency skills into his read aloud (see observation page in appendix).

How important is fluency? A low level of fluency may indicate a low level of comprehension. If a reader is not chunking the words into meaningful phrases, chances are he is not making much meaning of the text. Just as slurring my words and phrases together when speaking would confuse the listener, doing this during reading can prevent the meaning of the text from coming to life.

## Chapter 5: COMPREHENSION

"Even if a child is a proficient word-caller, the child also must be able to comprehend what is read" (McKenna & Stahl, 2003). When learning a new language, one of the first things we may learn to do is pronounce the words. If we were to see a line of text in the foreign language, we might be able to pronounce the words with confidence. Although we may be able to *say* the words, we may not have a clue what those words mean. The same is true of some young readers. They can read with high word accuracy but do not recall the meaning of the text. If a child can "bark" all the words, yet cannot remember or recall what he has just "barked", he is not really reading. Reading equals thinking. In this section, we are going to explore how to check for comprehension as well as examine a few factors that affect reading comprehension.

## Answering Questions and Question Prompt List for Fiction and Non-Fiction

### Answering Questions

One of the easiest ways to check for comprehension is to ask the child questions about the text he has just read. There are two basic kinds of questions that can be asked of a young reader:

1. **Explicit Questions (E).** These are literal types of questions for which the answers can be directly found in the text. Examples of this type of question may include: Who is the main character? What did the girl give the boy at the lunch table? Where did the story take place?

2. **Implicit Questions (I).** Implicit questions are those with less obvious answers. This requires the child to create his own answer by combining the words of text and his own knowledge. Examples of this type of question may include: Why do you think Mom threw out the garbage? How do you think the boy felt? What is the most interesting fact in that section?

Bloom's Taxonomy is a great place to start as far as question prompts to get you started. Bloom lists questions in six different levels: 1—knowledge, 2—comprehension, 3—application, 4—analysis, 5—synthesis, and 6—evaluation. The levels in Bloom's Taxonomy start with explicit questions and move into implicit questions as the levels increase. It is not my desire to dig deeply into each level but to simply show you how you can use question prompts to check your child's comprehension. I am pulling a few question prompts specifically for fiction and nonfiction texts from the different levels of Bloom's Taxonomy.

## Question Prompts for Fiction

### Explicit Questions:

- Who did that?
- What was the name...?
- What happened first? What happened after...?
- What is a characteristic of the main character?
- Which one...?
- Where did the story take place?
- Where was...?
- What was the problem in the story?

### Implicit Questions:

- What do you predict...?
- What does it mean...?
- Can you retell it in your own words?

- What was the turning point…?
- How did _____ feel when that happened?
- What image do you see in your head?
- Why do you think that character…? (characters' motives)
- Why was…?
- Why do you think…?
- Does this remind you of…?
- Do you think that character made a wise decision? Why/why not?
- What is the main idea of the story?
- Judge the title of the story. Would you change it or keep it?
- What questions would you ask the character if you could?
- What would have happened if…?
- How would you feel if…?
- What part of this story could/couldn't really happen?
- What is the moral of the story?
- What is the theme of the story?
- How would you have solved the problem differently?

**Question Prompts for Non-Fiction**

**Explicit Questions:**

- What is the passage mainly about?
- Name all the…?
- Name one way that…
- What is one example of…?
- According to your reading, what…?
- What is the first step in…?
- What are the conditions needed for…?
- Can you create a quick outline?

**Implicit Questions:**

- What was the most interesting fact?
- What was the most important idea?
- What does it mean…?
- Can you illustrate…?
- Describe the….

- Why did _____ happen?
- Why don't...?
- How would you compare and contrast...?
- How do you know that...?
- What does it mean when...?
- Can you explain...?
- What's a good definition of...?
- What are some problems of...?
- Do you think _____ is a good thing or bad thing? Why?
- Why do you think...?
- What would result if...?
- How effective are...?
- Why might some people dislike...?
- What is your opinion of...?
- What was the author's purpose in writing this text?
- Is that fact or fiction?
- Judge the title of the text. Would you change it or keep it?
- Why would it be a good idea to...?
- What would happen if...?
- What is your opinion of...?

Before you give the text to the child to read, it is important to read it over yourself. After you read the text, pick six to eight questions you'd like to ask your child (feel free to choose or adapt your questions from the prompts on the list above). Make sure that you get a good mixture of explicit and implicit questions. Note that in order for a child to answer many of the implicit questions, he'll need to understand the explicit. For example, if you asked the child a question like, "What would have happened if..." he would have to be able to comprehend and verbalize what literally happened before he could alter the outcome. (For more about asking questions, please read the "After Reading" section in Chapter 7.)

## Other Factors that Affect Comprehension

If the child struggles to answer questions after he reads (answering at less than 75% correct), he may be lacking some basic comprehension skills and strategies. The factors mentioned below must be considered when you pick out books for his reading instruction. His comprehension will be greatly affected (positively or negatively) by them. Because these particular factors are not the main subject of this book, I am going to provide basic background information. If the child struggles to comprehend, you will want to explore these further.

## Prior Knowledge and Vocabulary

## Prior Knowledge

Prior knowledge (or schema) is basically what the reader knows before reading the text. "[Prior knowledge] is all the stuff that's already inside your head, like places you've been, things you've done, books you've read—all the experiences you've had that make up who you are and what you know and believe to be true" (Miller, 2002). The reason it is so important is that a child's prior knowledge directly affects how well she comprehends texts. It is very difficult, even for adults, to pick up a book relating to a topic for which we have little to no background knowledge and comprehend it. Hand me a manual to install a light switch, and I go cross-eyed! "One of the biggest problems readers encounter when they read...is the need for background knowledge" (Calkins, 2001). Young readers need our support to comprehend texts by building up their schema or prior knowledge. When you pick a book for a child, consider how much prior knowledge he has about the topic.

## Vocabulary

Prior knowledge has a first cousin: vocabulary. When a reader comes to a text with lots of prior knowledge about the subject, it is typically easier for the child to comprehend because much of the vocabulary is familiar. If the reader is really into horses, you've probably read a lot about horses to her. She may be taking riding lessons and even know the parts of a horse. When she comes to a text about horses, much of the specific vocabulary related to horses will already be in her head because of her prior knowledge. When she comes to a word like *muzzle*, she may be able to read and comprehend it like it is second nature. On the flip side, when a child does not have a lot of prior knowledge about a particular subject, new vocabulary words are not only hard to decode but hard to comprehend. Although vocabulary breakdown can happen in fiction texts, it tends to happen more in non-fiction texts, when the vocabulary is unique to that particular subject.

**Comprehension Strategies**

This section covers the common comprehension strategies that your reader may be lacking.

**Making Connections**

Good readers make connections when they read, connecting the text to what they know (prior knowledge). It might sound like,

"Oh that's happened to me before…" or "I felt the same exact way when…."

**There are three different kinds of meaningful connections kids can make:**

1. text-to-self,
2. text-to-text, and
3. text-to-world.

## Predicting and Inferring

Predicting is probably the most familiar of all the comprehension strategies. It is actually a rather complicated strategy because it requires readers to use the clues the author gives them, tap into their own prior knowledge (making connections), and make an educated guess as to what might happen next. Many times, our predictions are not correct, and we constantly monitor and modify our predictions as we read on.

## Making Inferences

Inferring could simply be defined as "reading between the lines". It's what the reader can guess is going on, even if the author doesn't spell it out. Making inferences is highly related to making predictions, because it also requires the reader to combine text or picture clues and their own prior knowledge in a way that creates an inference about the text. Readers may have to infer the setting of the book, characters' feelings, the lesson or moral of the story, or the author's purpose.

## Asking Questions

One of the things that good readers do is ask themselves questions as they read. Questions can be asked for several reasons: 1) to clarify meaning, 2) as a springboard for other comprehension strategies, or 3) to propel the story forward. For example, a child may not understand a certain word in the book, asking himself, "What does that word mean?" In addition, the reader may ask, "Why did the author do that?", which will hopefully lead him to inferring the author's purpose. Questions such as "What will the character do next?" invite the reader to keep reading the story or text to find out.

## Making Mental Images

Visualizing helps readers to experience the text in ways that make it personal to them. No two people will hear the same text and envision it the same way. Visualizing also helps readers remember what they've read, because it attaches a vivid picture to the written word. Mental images can change as we read through the text (much like our predictions can change), creating a "movie in the mind".

## Determining Importance

It is vital for readers to be able to decipher important information from the not-so-important information when reading a text. Have you ever asked a child to quickly recap a story only to sit and listen as they begin to tell you every single detail? In general, it tends to be easier for young readers to figure out what is important in fiction because the text structure or story line is more familiar. Non-fiction is where many readers (even those who do not struggle) begin to get confused in determining what is important in text. It seems that sometimes the author throws loads of information at the reader, requiring the reader to figure out what to make of it. The reader must decipher not only what is important but also what is *not* important. Understanding the different nonfiction text features and structures is a big part of the solution. (See the next section for Text Features and Text Structures.)

## Synthesizing

When good readers read, their thinking grows as they process and progress through the text. They might initially think one thing as they begin reading only to have their initial thoughts challenged or added to later in the text. Debbie Miller likens it to throwing a rock into a pond: "first there's the splash, and then the water ripples out, making little waves that get bigger and bigger...as you read, your thinking evolves and the meaning gets bigger and bigger..." (Miller, 2002). A child may predict something based on the title or the picture on the front cover, but as the story unfolds, his prediction is revealed to be off-base. If he understands how to synthesize (add new information to his thinking), he will recognize this and change his prediction to one that makes more sense with the new information he has read. If he tries to hold on to his original prediction, even when faced with new information, the text will probably become difficult for him to comprehend.

## Text Organization for Fiction and Non-Fiction

### Fiction Story Elements and Text Structure

Studying the story elements and structure of fiction is an important way to deepen a child's reading comprehension because it helps them understand what is important. It also spills over nicely into helping them write their own fictional stories.

### Some fiction story elements include*

- characters: main characters and supporting characters,

- setting: when and where the story takes place,

- problem or conflict: usually introduced early on; can be external or internal,

- plot or text structure: the rise and fall of action,

- solution or resolution: how the problem or conflict is solved,

- point of view: 1st person (main character telling story; use of "I" and "me") or 3rd person (narrator telling story; use of "he/she", "him/her"), and

- theme: more than the topic of the story, the "message" the author is trying to send through the use of the story.

*Not all fiction works include all of these elements. Sometimes the plot is not organized and packaged so neatly. When I'm faced with texts such as these, I'll ask the reader to tell what happened first, next, and last. Then, we'll work on finding the main idea of the story. To describe the main idea, I use phrases such as "What was the story mainly about?" or "If you could tell me what the story was all about in two to three sentences, what would you say?"

**Fiction Text Structure**

Text structure simply refers to how the information in the text is organized. Knowing what kind of structure a text has helps readers to organize, comprehend, and summarize the important information within that text. With fiction, the structure refers to the story line or plot.

**Examples of fiction text structure are**

1. **Introduction:** includes the setting and characters and a problem,

2. **Rise in Action**: the character(s) works to solve the problem, often times faced with other obstacles along the way, and

3. **Fall in Action**: the character(s) has solved the problem; good usually "wins".

When young readers understand this simple structure, it gives them hooks on which to hang the events that happen in the story, making it much easier to retell. Conversely, if a child does not have those "hooks", comprehension is laborious.

**Non-Fiction Text Features and Text Structure**

**Text Features**

Text features within non-fiction are those special features authors have included to help readers understand the content. They include things like maps, special print, and charts. Without them, comprehension could be greatly compromised. For example, if the author wants a reader to understand where a country is in the world, providing a map helps the reader visualize and understand the importance of that country's location. If the anatomy of an animal is vitally important to understanding a text, a detailed photograph with labels gives the reader the support he needs to comprehend the text.

Text features also help readers determine what is important to the text and to them. Without a table of contents or an index, readers can spend wasted time flipping through the book to find the information they need. Special print helps draw the attention of the reader to important or key words and phrases.

**Some common text features within non-fiction are**

- Captions. These help you better understand a picture or photograph.

- Comparisons. These types of sentences help you to picture something. (Example: A whale shark is a little bit bigger than a school bus.)

- Glossary. This helps you define words that are in the book.

- Graphics. Charts, graphs, or cutaways are used to help you understand what the author is trying to tell you.

- Illustrations/Photographs. These help you to know exactly what something looks like.

- Index. This is an alphabetical list of ideas that are in the book. It tells you what page the idea is on.

- Labels. These help you identify a picture or a photograph and its parts.

- Maps. These help you to understand where places are in the world.

- Special print. When a word is bold, in *italics*, or <u>underlined,</u> it is an ***<u>important</u>*** word for you to know.

- Subtitles. These headings help you to know what the next section will be about.

- Table of Contents. This helps you identify key topics in the book in the order they are presented.

## Non-Fiction Text Structure

Once again, text structure refers to the format whereby the author chooses to portray the information within the text. Understanding non-fiction text structure is a bit more complicated, but they are just as important for young readers to learn. When readers know what kind of structure an author has used, it helps them to

- better connect to and remember what they've read better,

- understand what is important to the text, and

- summarize the text. If we are summarizing a text that has a sequence/time order structure, we want to make sure we summarize using the same structure. For example, it would not make sense to tell an autobiography out of order. We must retell it in sequence, as the material is presented in the text.

**Examples of non-fiction text structure are**

1. **Problem/Solution.** The author will introduce a problem and tell us how the problem could be fixed. There may be one solution to fix the problem or several different solutions mentioned.

2. **Cause and effect.** The author describes something that has happened which has had an effect on or caused something else to happen. It could be a good effect or a bad effect. There may be more than one cause and there may also be more than one effect. Many times, problem/solution and cause and effect seem like "cousins" because they can be together.

3. **Compare/Contrast.** The author's purpose is to tell you how two things are the same and how they are different by comparing them.

4. **Description/List.** Although this is a very common text structure, I think it's one of the trickiest because the author throws a lot of information at the reader (or lists facts) about a certain subject. It's up to the reader to determine what he thinks is important and interesting enough to remember.

5. **Time Order/Sequence.** Texts are written in an order or timeline format.

**Note:** Sometimes the text structure isn't so easy to distinguish. For example, the structure of the text as a whole may be Description/List (maybe about Crocodilians), but the author may devote one chapter to Compare/Contrast (Alligators vs. Crocodiles). When teaching text structure, we must be explicit about this with young readers by pointing this out and discussing it together.

## Chapter 6: HOW TO DETERMINE THE LEVEL OF A TEXT

You may be thinking, "This sounds great and all, but how do I pick up a text and know its level?" The answer is not as clear-cut as you would think. The reason for this is that there are multiple assessments for finding levels (such as DRA levels, Guided Reading Levels, Running Record Levels, Lexile Levels, and AR or grade level equivalents). Each assessment measure has its own "code" for leveling books, and the levels do not always match up.

Let's say you go to your favorite discount store and pick up a Level 1 reader. You might expect that a Kindergartener or first grader could read it. But many times, that Level 1 reader is too difficult. In the Appendix, I have provided a chart that demonstrates how these leveling systems match up side-by-side.

### Book Leveling Systems

Use the coding system the child's school uses or pick the one you feel the most comfortable with and stick with it. Start by leveling all the books in your collection for which you have a definite level with the kind of system you have chosen. There are some great resources online for doing this. Here are a few:

- AR Levels (http://www.arbookfind.com/UserType.aspx)

- Leveled Book Database from Beaverton School District. (https://leveledbooks.beaverton.k12.or.us/) Find books by Lexile, DRA Level, and Guided Reading Level. Texts are also searchable by title, author, publisher, and subject.

- Scholastic's Reading Counts (http://src.scholastic.com/bookexpert) Type in the book title to find the Lexile, Guided Reading Level, and Grade Level Equivalent (AR).

- Leveled Book Lists for Guided Reading Levels (http://home.comcast.net/~ngiansante/index.html) Search by book level according to the title or author.

- Reading Recovery Book Levels (http://users.oasisol.com/daireme/book.htm)

- Barnes & Noble (http://www.barnesandnoble.com/) or Amazon.com. If you are unable to find any of the books in the lists above, try it at the Barnes & Noble or Amazon websites. Scroll down to read the product information. Many times, there is a grade level or age level provided, which can give you a rough guide.

## Book Features to Consider

Once you have some of your books labeled according to their official level, begin looking at the other books in your collection. While skimming through these other books, look for certain features:

1. **Print size and spacing of the words.** Is the print very large or very tiny? How much space is given between words and lines of text? Books on a lower reading level tend to have larger print with more space between words and lines.

2. **The number of words and lines on each page.** Books for younger readers typically have fewer words and less lines of text on each page.

3. **The length of the sentences.** There is no magic formula, such as 5-10 words equals a Kindergarten text, but the length of sentences does get factored into the assessment of the text's level. Typically, books on higher levels have a longer sentence structure.

4. **The pictures.** How many pictures are included in the book? Do the pictures give the reader lots of help to figure out unknown words on the page?

5. **The sight words included.** Get out Fry's list of sight words and compare. If the text includes words in Fry's third hundred list, it probably will not work as a first grade text. (Fry's first 100 words should be mastered *by the end* of first grade, second 100 words should be mastered *by the end* of second grade, etc.) You can easily find Fry's list of words by searching "Fry's List of Sight Words" on the internet.

6. **The phonics features included.** If you are trying to decide if the book you have is a first grade text, expect to find first

grade phonics features (short vowel words, blends, digraphs, common long vowel words, etc.), not those phonics features of later grades. If you are unsure what phonics features should be covered in each grade level, talk with your child's teacher or look at a reading/phonics curriculum for that particular grade.

7. **The length and vocabulary of the words.** Words on a lower reading level are usually shorter, contain less syllables, and are more common words (*baby* is used instead of *infant*) while texts on a higher reading level tend to be more complex, containing multisyllabic words with suffixes.

8. **Topic of the book.** This book feature is subjective for each person, but I like to look at the content of the book. If the subject matter is for older kids (maybe about brutality in war), I tend to level it for older kids.

Leveling books by yourself can be overwhelming and intimidating. If you hit a bump (or two or three), ask a teacher from your child's grade level if she would give you her opinion or ask another parent who has a child the same age as yours. One of my favorite strategies is to compare the book in question to a book for which I already know the level. I look at all the features mentioned above to see how they are the same or different. If you are still unsure, another effective strategy is to give it to the child to read. After listening to him read the first couple of pages or so, you may be able to tell if you have approximated its level correctly. Please also note that Lucy Calkins (a reading teacher guru) says herself, "We rarely feel absolutely certain [that we have the exact level of a book], but our rule of thumb is that when we're not certain, we put a book in the higher level (which means it's more likely to be too easy than too hard)" (Calkins, 2001). What a great tip!

## Chapter 7: IT'S TIME TO ASSESS - Before, During, and After Reading Tips

Here is where we get to the nitty-gritty. Hang on, because it *will* be worth it! In this chapter, you will find helpful tips for preparing and implementing your reading assessment time.

**Before Reading**

**1. Locate text(s) that the child has not read (or heard) before.**

It is important to use texts that have not been used with your child before so you can get a "clean catch" of word recognition and comprehension. In my experience, asking a child to read just one book will not give you enough information to know that "just right" level right away. Several texts (and possibly texts on different grade levels) may need to be read before you can get the bigger picture. You will want to have a good mixture of fiction and nonfiction texts. If you know the child's approximate reading level, start on that level. If you do not know the child's approximate reading level, start with texts that are one grade level below his actual grade level. If the child is a struggling reader, you may need to start with a text that is two to three grade levels below his actual grade. For example, if he is in the second grade, start with a text on a Kindergarten grade level. It's better to start with a text that he will do well with than to start with a text that is at his frustration level.

**2. Count out the number of words you'd like the child to read aloud from the text.** I recommend finding a text (or a portion of text) that's anywhere between 40 words for young readers to 300 words for older readers. Please note that for older readers, it does not need to be the entire text. Choose a 300-word passage right out of the text. If you are using a chapter book, the passage will probably need to come from the first chapter instead of the middle of the book so comprehension is easier. Most nonfiction texts are structured in a way that choosing a 300-word passage from later in the book will be just fine.

**3. Type up the words or find a duplicate book to make it easy for you to follow along.** When administering a reading test like this, I do not like to share the text with the child. It can be nerve-wracking for a child to have an adult looking over his shoulder as he reads.

4. **Before the child ever reads a word, read it to yourself.** Jot down six to eight questions you can ask your child after he has read to check his comprehension. (Remember that "just right" levels are found by assessing word knowledge *and* comprehension.) Be sure you include some questions that require your child to do some thinking. If you need some question prompts, look over the question prompt list in Chapter 6.

5. **Prepare the child by explaining the following:**

- You want to get a good idea as to what kinds of books he can read and explore on his own and with you, so you need to listen to him read out loud. This may be intimidating, especially if the young reader has never done this before.

- You need him to read more than one text that day. One text rarely gives you all of the information you need to nail down that "just right" level. (I recommend stopping at three texts in each sitting, if you feel it will take several texts to get it figured out.)

- You will be timing him to see what his reading rate is, but you do not want him to try and beat a timer. You want his energy spent on making meaning as he reads. (If you use free apps like Audio Memos (apple) or Evernote (android), they will do the timing for you.)

- You will be recording him. This is where your phone or tablet comes in handy with those free apps. If you are new to this, I highly recommend recording the child's voice as he reads. Sometimes the mistakes kids make in a text get a little "messy". With a recording, you can go back later and repeat that section of reading over and over to ensure that your written record is an accurate reflection of his reading abilities.

6. **You will want to write down the things he does well while reading and the things he needs to work on.** This is why I suggest not sitting too close to your child as he may begin to

focus more on what you are writing than what he is reading. If you are new to taking notes, just sit and listen the first time (while recording), following along in your duplicate text. Marking up your text copy can be saved for when you listen to the recording, but you may want to jot down reading behaviors of the child. (See the next section for Reading Behaviors.)

7. **Give the book to your child, read the title, and give a *brief* introduction.** For example, with book *The Snowy Day* by Ezra Jack Keats, I might say, "Today you're going to read a book called *The Snowy Day*. Let's read to find out what the little boy does on the snowy day." (If the character's name is one that I do not think the child will be able to pronounce, such as Juan, I use the character's name in my introduction.) It is important to keep the introduction brief because you do not want to give away what happens in the book. Remember, if your child is already familiar with the book, you do *not* want to use it!

**During Reading**

There are three main things you want to keep track of while the child reads. This is why I highly recommend recording your child's reading so that you can keep track a little better.

- **Keep track of mistakes.** You will want to follow along, word for word, as he reads. I suggest following along with a duplicate copy of the text (whether you type it or have two copies of the text). Again, you may choose not to write anything in your text as he reads live, but instead wait until you have a chance to listen to the recording. Whether you mark the text while the child is reading live or later with a recording, this is where the miscues from Chapter 4 come into play. You will want to keep an accurate record of his mistakes so you can effectively determine his "just right" level. In the Appendix, you will find a chart with suggestions and examples on how to mark the child's mistakes. Note that these are just suggested ways to mark the text that your child is reading. Feel free to create your own system. As long as you are consistent, and it makes sense for you, go with it.

- **Keep track of reading behaviors.** While the child reads (or when listening to the recording), you will also want to make quick notes about reading behaviors, both for word recognition and understanding. For example, does the child re-read when the text does not make sense? I have included a reading behavior chart in the Appendix. Feel free to use a check system beside each behavior. If you are unsure of that particular behavior or it was not observed during the child's reading, simply leave it blank. This list is not meant to overwhelm you, but to help you organize your thoughts as you listen to and observe the child. You may want to write your own observations in the space provided below each chart.

- **Keep track of the number of seconds it took the child to read.** Whether you use an app or a stopwatch, you want to keep track of how many seconds it took the reader to read the passage. This will help you calculate how many words per minute the child reads. We will talk more specifically about how to calculate words per minute in the next chapter.

**After Reading**

- Once the child is finished reading the text, ask him to close the text and set it aside. You want to see what your child remembers without looking back. (Optional: you may want to allow the child to finish reading until the end of the text or the end of the section. For example, if you have chosen a 300-word passage from the first chapter in a book, you might want your child to finish reading the chapter before answering questions. This can be done out loud, or you can allow him to finish silently.)

- Ask the six to eight questions you prepared from when you read the text.

- *Please note that for our purposes, we are checking comprehension with these questions, not teaching it.* If the child does not know the answer, this is not the time to give him the answers. Sometimes, questions can be phrased differently, but be careful that you are not "leading the witness" with the way questions are phrased. For example, instead of asking, "What was the main idea of the passage?" you could rephrase it by asking, "What was the passage mostly about?"

- As the child gives his answers, jot down what he says. You can use the chart provided in the Appendix to write your questions as well as to write the child's answers.

- Note that implicit questions (questions that require readers to think a little deeper) may not have a "wrong" answer. As an example, the answer to, "What is your opinion about…" may differ from child to child. But the child's answer can give you a window into his understanding or lack of when it comes to comprehension. If his answer is supported by the ideas and details in the text, it is likely that he has a good understanding of the text. If, on the flip side, the reader's opinion is not supported by the ideas and details in the text, chances are his understanding is lacking in some way. If the child's answer leaves you wondering if he comprehends, a few follow-up questions may be needed such as "What from the text makes you think that?" or "Why do you think that?" or "Do you think the author of this text would agree with your opinion? Why or why not?"

- Once you are finished assessing the child's comprehension, you can revisit the questions he answered incorrectly, if you would like. To do this, hand the text back to him and re-ask one of the questions he did not answer correctly the first time. Ask him to open up the book to find the portion of text that will help him answer that question. If the child can do this successfully, mark that in your reading behavior notes, but do *not* count it as a correct answer when scoring his comprehension. If the child is unable to answer the question, even with a look-back, make notes about that as well. On the Comprehension Question Recording Sheet (in the Appendix), I have also provided a place where you can circle "look back" if you did this with the child.

## Chapter 8: PUTTING IT ALL TOGETHER - The Math Behind the Method

Once you have marked all the child's reading mistakes, calculated the number of seconds it took him to read, made some simple reading observations, and "graded" their comprehension questions, it's time to add some math to the method. Hang on again. I hope to make this as simple as possible!

**Calculating Word Accuracy, Comprehension, and Word Speed**

**Calculating Word Accuracy**

**To determine the percentage of words your child has read correctly from the text**

1. Subtract the number of mistakes from the number of words in the passage. This will give you the number of words the child read correctly.

2. Divide this number by the number of words in the passage. This will give you the percentage of words read correctly. The chart below gives an example:

| Percentage of Word Accuracy | |
|---|---|
| **First Subtract, then Divide** | **Example** |
| # of words in the passage | 150 words in the passage   1. subtract |
| — # of mistakes the child made | — 10 mistakes made |
| Divide this number by the # of words in the passage, which will equal the percentage read correctly | 140 words read correctly   2. divide |
| | 140 divided by 150 = 93% |

Be kind to yourself and use a calculator unless you really want to brush up on your long division!

**There are three word accuracy levels:**

- **Independent Level.** This is when child can read without help. Most guides suggest a word accuracy percentage of 98% or higher.

- **Instructional Level.** This is what I refer to as "just right" for instructional purposes and means that 95%-97% of words are read correctly.

- **Frustration Level.** This is when there is a 94% word accuracy or lower.

## Calculating Comprehension

To calculate comprehension, divide the number of correct answers by the number of questions asked. If you asked four questions and three were answered correctly, then the percentage correct would be 75%. The more questions you can ask, the better accuracy you'll have in calculating your numbers. For instance, by only asking four questions, one wrong answer knocks the child down to the instructional level.

### There are three comprehension levels:

- **Independent Level.** This is when the child is able to comprehend without help—a score of 90% or higher.

- **Instructional Level.** This is what I refer to as "just right" for instructional purposes—75%-89% of questions answered correctly.

- **Frustration Level.** This is when the comprehension score is 74% or lower.

**Calculating Word Speed**

# Calculate Words Per Minute

$$\frac{\text{\# of words in the passage x 60}}{\text{actual time in seconds}}$$

A simple way to calculate words per minute is to take the number of words in the passage and multiply it by 60. Divide that number by the actual time *in seconds* it took for the child to read that passage. If the passage was 200 words long and Samantha read it in two minutes, her words per minute would be 100 words per minute. Take a look at the chart in Chapter 4 for suggested reading rates by the *grade level of the text,* not the grade level of the child. If the reader is in the fourth grade and reading a text at the second grade level, words per minute should be considered for the second grade level (the level of the text). "If [the child's] reading rate is noticeably outside of their desired range, there is work to be done" (Eckenwiler & Eckenwiler, 2007).

## Combining Your Calculations with Observations to Determine "Just Right"

When you are finally ready to determine that "just right" level, you want to look closely at two things:

1. the percentage level of **word accuracy** (either independent, instructional, or frustration) and

2. the percentage level of **comprehension** (either independent, instructional, or frustration).

Even though these numbers are quite objective, picking that "just right" level can be a bit subjective at times. When the lines seem a little gray (you are not sure between an independent or instructional level, for example), keep in mind those reading behavior notes and how quickly the child read the passage (words per minute). If the numbers seem to place the child at an independent level but his words per minute were quite a bit below the "normal" level and his reading sounded very choppy, I would lean more towards instructional level.

Here is a quick-reference chart to help you figure out Overall Levels of reading:

### Determining Overall Reading Levels

| Word Accuracy Level | | Comprehension Level | | Overall Level* |
|---|---|---|---|---|
| Independent Level | + | Independent Level | = | Independent Level |
| Instructional Level | + | Instructional Level | = | Instructional Level |
| Frustration Level | + | Frustration Level | = | Frustration Level |
| Independent Level | + | Instructional Level | = | Instructional Level |
| Instructional Level | + | Independent Level | = | Instructional Level |

*Please note that if either the Word Accuracy OR Comprehension Level is on Frustration Level, the Overall Level will be Frustration Level. Both Word Accuracy *and* Comprehension have to be Instructional Level or above in order to prevent frustration for the young reader.

Adapted from McKenna & Stahl (2003)

## I Know How to Select the "Just Right" Level. Now What?

Just to clarify once again, when I say, "just right", I'm referring mainly to the child's instructional level. This is the level of text that should be used for teaching purposes. This level will grow the young reader in both word accuracy and comprehension strategies because it fits his level of development. A text at a child's instructional level will be just enough out of reach that he cannot do it by himself. But once the child is given a little bit of guidance, he can do it. The hope is that these new skills will continue to grow so the text that was once on his instructional level will be at an independent level after guidance and practice.

It is important to keep in mind the young reader's *actual* grade level. For example, if the child is reading on a second grade level but is in the fifth grade, be sure to include read aloud texts on the fifth grade level. "Struggling readers [also] need access to grade-level material through a variety of experiences so they are exposed to grade-level ideas, text structures, and vocabulary" (Valencia & Buly, 2004).

Texts on a child's independent level (or too easy level) should be used during times when the teacher or parent is not available to help. These might include times such as silent reading, homework, and leisure reading.

Once you are made more aware of the young reader's levels of ability, it is important to help the young reader become more aware as well. This does *not* mean that you need to share with your already struggling third grader that he can only read on a first grade level. This only serves to shame the child and decrease motivation. Instead, teach the child how to pick up a text and size it up for himself. Included in the Appendix is a "Just Right" Books Printable Guide for use with the child to help him pick "just right" books.

## In Conclusion

Finding a child's "just right" level is attainable for anyone working with young readers. It can be such a satisfying experience for both the adult and the reader. Readers working on their "just right" level learn reading and comprehension skills that are beneficial for their reading development and growth. As I have shown throughout this book, listening to the child read, making observations, and calculating *both* word accuracy and comprehension is the most accurate way to find that "just right" level. While this involves more work than the simple five-finger rule mentioned in the Introduction, the process is well worth your time. Your young reader's success as a confident and independent reader is well worth it, too!

## APPENDIX
# Extra Charts and Printable Resources

Grade/Book Level Chart for K-5 (Chapter 6)

Marking the Reader's Mistakes (Chapter 7)

Reading Behavior Checklists (Chapter 7)

Assessment Text Form (Chapter 7)

Comprehension Question Recording Sheet (Chapter 7)

"Just Right" Books Printable for Kids (Chapter 8)


## Please go to http://bit.ly/1esE6gC to print out the full-sized versions of these resources.

(That is a shortened link. The full-length link is

http://thisreadingmama.com/wp-content/uploads/2014/01/Printable-Resource-

Pack-by-Becky-Spence-PDF.pdf.)

### Grade / Book Level Chart for K - 5

| Actual Grade Level | DRA | Guided Reading Level | Lexile Level | Grade Level Equivalent (A/R) | Reading Recovery |
|---|---|---|---|---|---|
| K | A-1 | A | - | K | 1 |
| K | 1 | B | - | .5 | 2 |
| K | 2 | C | | 1.0 | 3-4 |
| 1 | 3 | D | Up to 300L | 1.1 | 5-6 |
| 1 | 4 | E | Up to 300L | 1.2 | 7-8 |
| 1 | 6-8 | F | Up to 300L | 1.4 | 9-10 |
| 1 | 10 | G | Up to 300L | 1.5 | 1.5 |
| 1 | 12 | H | Up to 300L | 1.7 | 1.7 |
| 1 | 14 | I | Up to 300L | 1.8 | 15,16,17 |
| 2 | 16 | J | 140L to 500L | 2.0 | 18 |
| 2 | 20 | K | 140L to 500L | 2.3 | 18 |
| 2 | 24 | L | 140L to 500L | 2.6 | 20 |
| 2 | 28 | M | 140L to 500L | 2.9 | 20 |
| 3 | 30 | N | 330L to 700L | 3.0 | 22 |
| 3 | 34 | O | 330L to 700L | 3.3 | 24 |
| 3 | 38 | P | 330L to 700L | 3.6 | 24 |
| 4 | 40 | Q | 445L to 810L | 4.0 | 26 |
| 4 | 40 | R | 445L to 810L | 4.3 | 26 |
| 4 | 44 | S | 445L to 810L | 4.6 | 26 |
| 4/5 | 44 | T | | 4.8 | 26 |
| 5 | | U | 565L to 910L | 5.0 | 28 |
| 5/6 | | V | 565L to 910L | 5.3 | 28 |

## Marking the Reader's Mistakes

| The Text Says | The Child Reads | Mark It As |
|---|---|---|
| The monkeys sat in the tree. | "The monkeys in the tree." *leaving out or skipping words (omissions)* | The monkeys ~~sat~~ in the tree. |
| The monkeys sat in the tree. | "The monkeys sat up in the tree." *adding extra words (insertions)* | The monkeys sat $\wedge$ in the tree. *(up)* |
| The monkeys sat in the tree. | "The monkeys sit in the tree." *replacing word(s) / making substitutions* | The monkeys <u>sat</u> in the tree. *(sit)* |
| The monkeys sat in the tree. | "The the monkeys sat in the tree." *repeating a word or phrase* | <u>The</u> monkeys sat in the tree. |
| The monkeys sat in the tree. | "The (pause) monkeys sat in the tree." *hesitation or pause* | The / monkeys sat in the tree. |
| The monkeys sat in the tree. They watched the zookeeper clean up. | "The monkeys sat in the tree they watched the zookeeper clean up." *reading through punctuation* | The monkeys sat in the tree. They watched the zookeeper clean up. |
| The monkeys sat in the tree. | "The monkey sat in the (pause) monkeys sat in the tree." *self-corrections* | The monkeys sat in the / tree. *(SC, ~~money~~)* |
| The monkeys sat in the tree. | "The (long pause) ...." *parent supplied the word\** | The ~~monkeys~~ sat in the tree. *(P)* |

*Some reading assessments say not to supply any words, no matter how long the pause, but to encourage the child to skip the word. I typically supply the word after about 5 seconds of hesitation by the reader.

# Reading Behavior Checklists

These checklists are povided to help you keep a good record of reading behaviors, both for word recognition and comprehension. A check system can be used to help you keep track:

✓+ makes great use of this strategy

✓ average use of this strategy

✓- needs imporvement with the strategy

| Check | Word Identification and Fluency Behaviors |
|---|---|
|  | pauses or stops at punctuation |
|  | reads fluently, with proper phrasing |
|  | uses voice inflection (voice goes up or down as appropriate) |
|  | makes mistakes that make sense within the text |
|  | recognizes many words accurately and automatically when reading |
|  | reads at a normal rate for the grade-level of the text (check wpm chart) |
|  | rereads and self-corrects mistakes that do not make sense |
|  | figures out most unknown words without help from parent/teacher |

More Observation Notes:

| Check | Comprehension and Understanding Behaviours |
|---|---|
|  | has sufficient prior knowledge about the topic |
|  | goes back and re-reads text when meaning is lost |
|  | monitors understanding while reading |
|  | demonstrates use of one or more comprehension strategies while reading |
|  | is able to answer explicit questions about the text after reading |
|  | is able to answer implicit questions about the text after reading |
|  | can name examples from the text to support his answers/thinking |
|  | if provided the chance, can return to the text to find the answer |

More Observation Notes:

# Assessment Text Form

Re-type the text and print onto this paper. Once you have finished "grading" the assessment passage, fill in all the information in the box at the bottom.

| | |
|---|---|
| Text Title: | # of Seconds it took to Read \| wpm: |
| Estimated Grade Level of Text: | # of Mistakes Made \| % correct: |
| Fiction Nonfiction (circle one) | # of Questions Correct \| % correct: |
| # of Words in Passage: | Independent Level / Instrurctional Level / Frustration Level (circle one) |

75

# Comprehension Question Recording Sheet

Record your questions (six to eight total), circle explcit or implicit, then record the child's answers in the space provided. If you used the look-back feature with incorrect answers, circle *look back*.

Question 1: _____

Explicit / Implicit                                                    look back


Child's Answer:



Question 2: _____

Explicit / Implicit                                                    look back


Child's Answer:



Question 3: _____

Explicit / Implicit                                                    look back


Child's Answer:



Question 4: _____

Explicit / Implicit                                                    look back


Child's Answer:

## Comprehension Question Recording Sheet

Record your questions (six to eight total), circle explcit or implicit, then record the child's answers in the space provided.  If you used the look-back feature with incorrect answers, circle *look back*.

**Question 5:** _____

Explicit / Implicit                                                    look back

Child's Answer:

**Question 6:** _____

Explicit / Implicit                                                    look back

Child's Answer:

**Question 7:** _____

Explicit / Implicit                                                    look back

Child's Answer:

**Question 8:** _____

Explicit / Implicit                                                    look back

Child's Answer:

Too Easy

## A book is too easy when

● I know all the words,

● I make no mistakes when I read it,

● I've read it a lot of times, and/or

● I have it memorized.

Too Hard

## A book is too hard when

● there are a lot of words I don't know,

● I can't figure out the words I don't know,

● the topic is not familiar to me, and/or

● it does not make sense to me.

"Just Right"

## A book is "just right" when

● I know most of the words,

● I can figure out words I don't know,

● The topic is familiar to me,

● I am interested in what I'm reading, and/or

● I can understand what I'm reading.

## RESOURCES

Allington, Richard L. (2006). *What Really Matters for Struggling Readers*. Portland, ME:
   Pearson Education, Inc.


Bear, et al. (2004). Words Their Way. Portland, ME: Pearson Education, Inc.


Calkins, Lucy M. (2001). The Art of Teaching Reading. New York: Addison-Wesley
   Educational Publishers Inc.


Eckenwiler & Eckenwiler. (2007). Fluency. The Struggling Reader, Inc.
   (www.thestrugglingreader.com)


Leslie & Caldwell. (2006). Qualitative Reading Inventory IV. Portland, ME: Pearson Education,
   Inc.


McKenna & Stahl. (2003). Assessment for Reading Instruction. New York: The Guilford Press.


Miller, Debbie. (2002). Reading with Meaning. Portland, ME: Stenhouse Publishers.


Morris, Darrell. (2005). The Howard Street Tutoring Manual. New York: The Guilford Press.


Valencia, SW. & Buly, M.R. (2004). Behind Test Scores: What Struggling Readers Really Need.
   The Reading Teacher, 57(6), 520-521.

## ABOUT THE AUTHOR

Becky Spence traded in her public school teaching career to follow God's call to be at home with her children. As a stay-at-home mom, she finished her M.Ed. in Elementary Reading and tutored struggling readers in her home. In the fall of 2010, Becky began homeschooling. She knew this was God's call on her life, and after wrestling with it a bit, she felt at peace. But homeschooling was a little lonelier than expected. She desired to share her ideas and connect with other educators and parents. In February of 2011, she started her literacy blog, *ThisReadingMama.com*, where she shares practical tips, hands-on activities, printables, and reading curricula. You can connect with her on Google+, Pinterest, Facebook, Twitter, or subscribe by email to This Reading Mama.